LUCIANO BERTI

ALL THE WORKS OF
MICHELANGELO

Bonechi Edizioni -IL TURISMO- - FIRENZE

© 1969 © 1991 © 1994 by Bonechi Edizioni "Il Turismo" S.r.l.
Via dei Rustici, 5 - 50122 Florence
Tel. (055) 239.82.24 - Fax (055) 21.63.66
Printed in Italy
All rights reserved
Translation: Richard Peroni
Reproductions: La Fotolitografia, Florence
Printing: Lito Terrazzi, Florence
ISBN 88-7204-026-4

INDEX TO THE WORKS

MICHELANGELO BUONARROTI

The baby born on March 6th 1475, in the house of the Mayor of Caprese, a small settlement amidst the rough mountains of the upper Tiber valley, was destined for a long life. Until 1564, in fact. Remarkably, he would be seen by his contemporaries as the greatest artist of all time, in all three disciplines, superior even to those of Antiquity. Consequently, he acquired an almost mythical reputation, often called "divine". This, especially in the golden century of the Renaissance, was an extraordinary achievement due, no doubt, to Michelangelo's obsessive singlemindedness. He was an introvert, yet still had the world at his feet.

Vasari and Condivi tell of a solitary man with an extremely modest lifestyle – one of continuous, reclusive work. He was often measured and equivocal in conversation, but could add a cutting edge when required. Even though successful and fulfilled, he could often be unassuming and loving, but those who did not like him considered him a recluse, a mean, proud and enigmatic man. The fiercely proud Pope Julius II said, in 1512, to Sebastian del Piombo: "Michelangelo is so haughty that no-one can get close to him".

His life was frugal; the house was almost bare, and sometimes he ate only bread, working continuously. A note of three menus, from 1517, survive – one for himself, two for when he had guests: 1) Two pieces of bread, a decanter of wine, a herring, tortellini (pasta); 2) A salad, four pieces of bread, a decanter of "tondo", and a quart of sharp wine, a small plate of spinach, four anchovies, tortellini; 3) Six pieces of bread, two fennel soups, a herring, a decanter of "tondo".

Sustained, however, by his vision and prepared to work very hard for his art, Michelangelo created his own mystery. He channelled all his energies into his work, showing little consideration for the outside world. Indeed, all the world could see were his considerable achievements. For Michelangelo, such singlemindedness was something greater than just worldly ambition. He made no attempt, for example, to win the support of Aretino, the most respected commentator of the period. Even the possibility of great wealth did not distract him. He shunned connections with influential people and, even in 1549, at the height of his fame, he could write to his nephew Leonardo looking for recommendations. "I have very few contacts in Rome, and do not know those who can be of help. Should I ask something of any of them, they will require so much more from me. However, I need a few contacts, so will do all I can".

Nevertheless, Michelangelo knew how to cultivate his own myth. His fierce pride brought him the respect of those in high authority who were more used to the obsequious servility of others. Isolated and insular, he was seen as the Artist and nothing else. Aretino wrote of him: "... you, who would be divine, shun the company of men..." Equally, the well-known unfinished quality of his sculpture was perhaps a way of never having the final word on what constitutes unparalleled beauty. He made a bonfire of his drawings, wrote Vasari, "so that no one could see the effort that went into his work and the development of his skills, lest they see something imperfect..." His whole being was an immense expressive force, like the torment reflected in his unfinished statues; his only communion with others being through the imperious quality of his masterpieces.

Michelangelo's father, Ludovico, was a man of little ability. At best, he became a minor state official, when he was appointed Mayor of Caprese. Yet the Buonarroti Simoni family were of noble stock and had once been eminent Florentines. Understandably, Michelangelo thus determined to improve the family fortunes. "We are citizens of very noble descent", he loved to repeat, and so from 1506 he set out to buy land, deposit savings, and to arrange his nephews' marriages with aristocratic families. His nephew Leonardo would have had a significant inheritance, and the Buonarroti house in the ancestral quarter of Santa Croce is evidence of the artist's benevolence to his family. His mother, Francesca, died when Michelangelo was only six years old; perhaps the lack of feminine influence in his early years was later reflected in his portrayals of the Madonna. Michelangelo was steered towards literary studies but soon, in spite of opposition from his family, who considered an artistic career a lowly pursuit, he was drawn increasingly toward the latter.

THE FIRST WORKS: *The Madonna of the Steps -*
The Battle of the Centaurs - The Wooden Crucifix.

In 1488, aged thirteen, and possibly on the advice of the young painter Francesco Granacci, Michelangelo was placed for three years in the school of the famous artist Ghirlandaio. He did not receive any special attention there, and left after a year to study in the San Marco garden of Lorenzo the Magnificent, with its splendid collection of antique statues. The Curator at this time was the old sculptor Bertoldo. The Magnificent actually welcomed Michelangelo into the Medici Palace, amid the associates and intellectual circle that formed the court of the Lord of Florence. It was at this time, according to biographers, that Michelangelo produced two works which survive to this day: The *Madonna of the Steps* and the *Battle of the Centaurs.*

In the *Madonna* (fig. 1), the "schiacciato" (squashed) technique was borrowed from Donatello, but the draped figure of the Virgin is inspired by classical styles. The solidly-built Virgin draped in voluminous robes is seated, dominating the bas-relief, seemingly absorbed in thought. The children in the background, playing on the steps, are already holding the funeral sheet of the future Christ. The composition is tight, one image within another: the Madonna within the background; the back of the sturdy child, typically Michelangelesque, sitting on his mother's lap suckling the milk. Even in his early sketches, Michelangelo demonstrates his instinct towards powerful, cast figures, copying them from the earlier masters of Florentine art, Giotto and Masaccio.

The *Battle of the Centaurs* (fig. 2), the theme of which was suggested to the boy by Poliziano, clearly foreshadows his later style: it does not try to accurately reflect the scene of the title, but presents a whirling tangle of bodies, just a sample of the varied dynamic possibilities of the nude; equally, here (as well as in the Madonna) the work displays an unfinished quality (as in the thinly sketched heads of hair). This young protegé of Lorenzo the Magnificent therefore already displayed in these two marbles an art very different from the exquisite but more refined fifteenth-century elegance – a vision more powerful, more radical, more idealised.

When Lorenzo the Magnificent died in 1492, Michelangelo returned to his parental home. At this time, he favoured the teachings of Savonarola which prophesied a violent retribution for sinners, and called for a reform of the church. Religious feeling, the contrast between this and the paganism of classical culture, and the prospect of a Christian revival, were all notions that hardened within him during his lifetime. For the moment, though, he was experimenting in modelling the human form, as in the recently-discovered wooden *Crucifix* for S. Spirito (fig. 4), motivated more by his anatomical studies than any dramatic spiritual revolution invoked by Savonarola. Indeed, the Prior of S. Spirito provided for Michelangelo both a room and the bodies necessary for dissection. The Crucifix of S. Spirito, nevertheless, is slightly effeminate in style. From this period (1492-4) there was also a statue of Hercules, which ended up in France, and was lost.

THE FIRST FLIGHT FROM FLORENCE: *The Angel with Candelabrum - The Bacchus - The Pietà for St. Peter's.*

Michelangelo was very sensitive to the political disorder in Florence at this time, and when a renewed threat to the hated Piero dei Medici emerged in October 1494, he cautiously abandoned the house of his benefactors, and fled from the city. We find written: "It is known that Michelangelo the sculptor from the Garden went to Venice without saying anything to Piero... it seems to me that Piero took it badly". From Venice, he soon moved to Bologna where he spent a year as guest of the gentleman G.F. Aldrovandi. Michelangelo would read to him from the great Tuscan poets (Dante, Petrarch, Boccaccio), and through this gentleman's patronage came to sculpt a serene youthful *Angel* (fig. 3) for Niccolo dell'Arca's tomb of S. Domenico, along with statues of the Saints Petronius and Proculus, reflecting the vigorous style of Jacopo della Quercia.

At the end of 1495, Michelangelo returned to Florence where the situation had calmed somewhat. He only stayed six months, though, then moved on to Rome, where he remained until 1501. He did not work for the Papal Court of the Borgia Alexander VI, but made contact with Cardinal Riario, the banker Jacopo Galli (with whom perhaps he lived) and with the French Cardinal of S. Dionigi. Galli acquired the Bacchus, and the Cardinal of S. Dionigi commissioned, in 1498, the Pietà now at St. Peter's. Michelangelo's reputation must by now have been considerable, since Galli was able to give the following guarantee for the Pietà: "And I Jacopo Gallo promise the very reverend Monsignore that the said Michelangelo will complete the said work within a year, and it will be the most beautiful work of marble that there is today in Rome; no one is better than this master". Indeed, both the Bacchus and the Pietà are clearly masterpieces; Michelangelo signed the Pietà, which he did not do on any other work, as a sign of his complete satisfaction.

These two works reflect a creative contrast – one profane, one sacred – that had already been seen with the Battle of the Centaurs and the Madonna of the Steps. In the *Bacchus* (fig. 5) there is a pagan, turgid, enigmatic physical beauty. Vasari speaks of Michelangelo "having given it the lightness of male youth and the fleshiness and roundness of a girl". There is a feeling of genuine sensuality in the swaying pose and the drunken face of the young god which is most effective. Yet, the composition begs to be seen from several viewpoints around the statue, and there is a wealth of sweeping lines that come together in the satyr, stealing the grapes from behind the god's back. There is also a definite symbolic representation of downfall and renewal: the god holds a tiger's skin, the animal dedicated to Bacchus which, greedy for the grapes and the wine, dies. The merry satyr completes the cycle, illustrating sensual pleasures and the joy of life.

In the *Pietà*, however, (figs. 7,8) a youthful Madonna sits totally absorbed in her grief, her left hand indicating a resignation to God's will. The beautiful body of the dead Christ, head inclined backwards, lays across her knees; splendid drapery cascades over her lap. The figure of the Virgin reflects a Leonardesque sweetness;

A copy from Giotto.

yet the intricacy of every detail places it in the Florentine Quattrocento. It seems that Buonarroti was not yet ready to sacrifice beauty in favour of drama and vigorous energy, and this is reflected in contemporary criticisms that his Virgin is so impossibly youthful, so unrealistic, that he has favoured the beauty of the grouping over all other considerations. Who would have predicted that Michelangelo could later create the *Rondanini Pietà* (fig. 70)?

THE YOUTHFUL MASTERPIECES IN FLORENCE: *The Bruges Madonna - The Pitti Tondo - The Taddei Tondo - The Doni Tondo - The David.*

From 1501 to 1505, Michelangelo returned to Florence. Leonardo was also there then, having returned from Milan, and Buonarroti, perhaps stimulated by the comparison with the great Da Vinci, now moved on to a more monumental phase. Putting to one side the statuettes for the Piccolomini altar in Siena (another commission of Galli), the series of works in this period include a statue of the Madonna and Child (Bruges), two sculptured "tondi" on the same theme (Bargello and the Royal Academy in London), one painted "tondo" (Uffizi), a bronze David, now lost, and the gigantic marble one, now at the Accademia in Florence, which should have been the first in a series of Apostles for the facade of the Duomo. Finally, there was a cartoon of "The Battle of Cascina", intended as a fresco for the Palazzo Vecchio, which is now lost, and which was created in competition with Leonardo's "Battle of Anghiari". At twenty-five years of age, Michelangelo was clearly able to stand alongside the fifty-year-old da Vinci. Stendhal remarked that: "The sculptor's fervent genius approached the task with an energy which pleased his admirers; they preferred Michelangelo who worked fast, to Leonardo who always kept promising..."

The *Bruges Madonna* (fig. 6), with the standing Child held back against the seated but rather erect figure of the Virgin, can be linked with the Pietà in St. Peter's, but displays much more severe blocking. The sculpture was sold in 1506 to the Mascheroni or Mouscron family, who transferred it to Bruges, where Dürer saw it in 1521. In the *Pitti Tondo* at the Bargello (fig. 12) and in the *Taddei Tondo*, now in London (fig. 14) the representation of the Madonna, not as a half-bust (which was traditional in the fifteenth century) but in complete form required a seated but oblique posture, with the curving lines of the Infants following the roundness of the marble form. Indeed, the tondo form gracefully brings together the individual tensions within the piece. The Madonnas do not display the overt sweetness of Leonardo, nor the harmonious serenity which Raphael painted while in Florence between 1504 and 1508. Yet the embossed, vibrant forms create proud and restless images. The marble is worked with great skill and confidence, rough and sketched in parts, finely detailed in others, creating diverse pictorial effects.

Study for Madonna and St. Anne.

In the *Tondo* painted for the *Doni* family (fig. 13), the composition of the Holy Family group is complex, and creates a spiral of movement that causes the eye to travel around the picture. In the background, a semicircle of nude youths alludes to an earlier paganism, and acts as a foil to the group in the foreground. Michelangelo contrasts Leonardo's mistyness and Raphael's sweetness with a very clear, precise quality of painting and bold, dynamic figures. Hard, emphatic colours and firm modelling in light and shade produce a unique sense of muscular energy. The celebrated *David* (figs. 10-11) was produced between 1501 and 1504. It was, miraculously, carved from one block of marble, with no additions. It had been started and then abandoned forty years before at the Office of Works of the Duomo, no one being capable of its completion. Thus Michelangelo's deeply-rooted pride found expression as a symbol of self-esteem for the city of Florence. In fact, the David symbolises the two civil virtues of "strength" (a harmonious yet powerful body, closed on its right side, open on its left with leg extended and arm bent to carry the sling) and "anger" (in the watchful and resolute face). Only on inspecting the flank can we appreciate the difficulties that Michelangelo had to overcome, the shallowness of the block necessitating a purely frontal figure. Finally, in his cartoon for "The Battle of Cascina", Michelangelo chose for his theme the moment when Florentine soldiers were startled by the alarm while bathing in the Arno. This composition totally comprises nudes springing up in various postures, thus concentrating solely on the human figure for its theme, in contrast to Leonardo's much wider treatment. These studies of the human form, both powerful and heroic, were to greatly influence artists of succeeding generations, and had a profound effect on sixteenth-century painting. Vasari noted that: "many artists, now either senile or dead, were affected, seeing the potential for art in such a work as Michelangelo showed them". Indeed, the cartoon was destroyed as various artists subsequently appropriated pieces of it as relics.

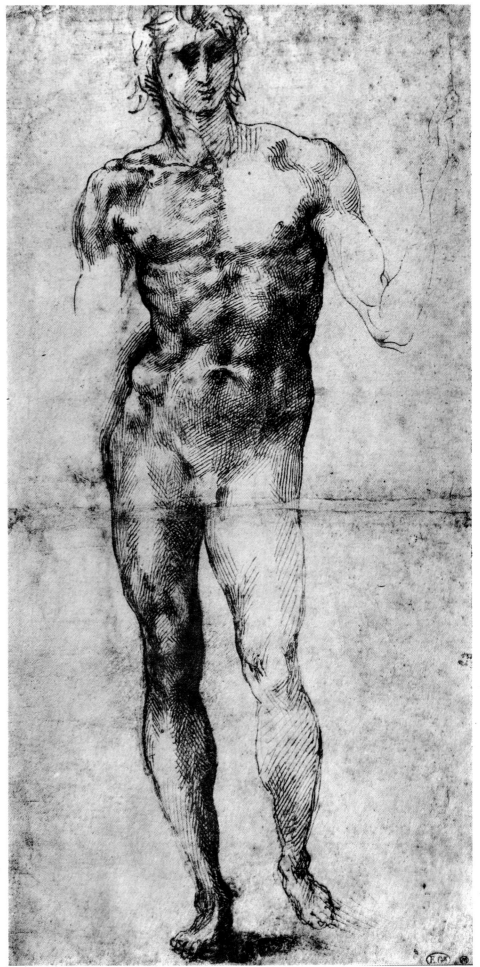

Study for a male figure.

Study for a figure for The Battle of Cascina.

THE MEETING WITH POPE JULIUS II:
The Project for the Pope's Sepulchre - The St. Matthew - The Sistine Chapel.

It was probably Giuliano da Sangallo, the Vatican architect, who recommended Michelangelo to Pope Julius II. Called to Rome in 1505, the Pope entrusted him with the project for his imposing *Sepulchre* (fig. 30), the tomb that the artist was to complete, much reduced in scale, some forty years later and which, to Michelangelo, became a life-long tragedy. Initially, however, the project – a gigantic, four-sided monument on three floors, with over forty figures – seemed to take shape quickly. Michelangelo took himself off at once to extract the necessary marbles from Carrara where eight months soon passed, as he daydreamed, among other things, of sculpting a colossus on a mountainside, visible to sailors miles away. The marbles for the sepulchre had already arrived in Rome when Michelangelo, considering himself offended by the Pontiff, abandoned it (17th August 1506) and fled to Florence, followed in vain by the Papal emissaries.

In November, Michelangelo presented himself before the Pope in Bologna, obtaining his pardon. Earlier, though, frightened at the prospect of incurring the Pope's wrath, he had even planned to emigrate to Turkey, where the Sultan offered him the job of building a great bridge for Constantinople. While in Florence, he had produced the *St. Matthew* (fig. 15), an unfinished figure emerging from the rough block which imprisons it, the face and demeanour of the visionary dramatic in its sense of freedom. In Bologna, after the reconciliation, Julius II commissioned from him a bronze statue for the facade of St. Petronio, seated and in the act of benediction, which the artist cast in 1507 and which was destroyed by the Bolognese when they rebelled in 1511.

In 1506, however, Pope Julius had thought of commissioning Buonarroti to fresco the vault of the Sistine Chapel. Michelangelo was perhaps reluctant initially to abandon the pontifical sepulchre, and to experiment with a pictorial technique of which he had little experience. In the Spring of 1508, however, the job was accepted and the artist was soon enthusiastically proposing a project – subsequently welcomed – much more complex than before. He called some helpers to Florence, among them his old friend Granacci, but it was not long before he dismissed them and carried on alone, completing the work in twenty months. The preparation of the drawings and cartoons continued until January 1509; in October 1512 all was finished. On the *Chapel ceiling* (figs. 16-27) Michelangelo laid out an imposing, powerful structure of false architecture, enlivened by some three hundred figures, and nine scenes from Genesis which can be seen on the open pictures at the apex of the vault. On the other side of the apex, Michelangelo's personal vision on an heroic scale is evident: gigantic figures of *Sibyls* and *Prophets* (figs. 20-27), seated at the base of the vault, their physical monumentality reflecting a certain spirituality. Couples of beautiful nude youths provide movement to the scenes above, adding animation of the highest quality. The biblical scenes become ever more grand as we advance toward the altar end of the

Chapel, to the very first scenes where the principal performer is the Creator himself. Perhaps the supreme scene is the *Creation of Adam* (fig. 18) where the Almighty, through the contact of hands, gives life – as in an electric current – to the powerful but still torpid body of the first man created by Him. To the sides, and at the base of the pendentives and the lunettes (showing the ancestors of Christ) the paintings reveal a more instictive characterisation and are more inspired, intimate and humorous. In a sketch at the Casa Buonarroti, we can see Michelangelo's own caricature of himself painting the difficult frescoes – head held upwards – on the immense vault (over 1000 sq. metres). It is accompanied by a satirical outburst in verse:

> *"I've got a goitre from this strain*
> *just as cats do from the water in Lombardy..."*

which ends in a pessimistic and disconsolate tone:

> *"Giovanni, come to the rescue*
> *Of my dead painting now, and of my honour;*
> *I'm not in a good place, and I'm no painter."*

Study for an old man's head.

Study for a head.

18

THE TOMB OF JULIUS II AND THE WORKS FOR THE MEDICI PONTIFFS IN FLORENCE:
The Louvre Prisoners - Moses - The Prisoners (at the Accademia) - Victory - The Facade of San Lorenzo - The New Sacristy - The Risen Christ - Biblioteca Laurenziana

Julius II died unexpectedly in 1513. His sepulchre, therefore, suddenly became necessary. Michelangelo's rivals had often tried to dissuade him from the project, suggesting that it was inauspicious, but the same year Buonarroti signed a new contract for the work with the executors of the will. Between 1513 and 1516 he created two *Prisoners* (figs. 28, 29), now in the Louvre, figures which symbolise the fettering of Art after the death of the Pontiff. Their torment reflects the then recently-discovered Laocoon, where the spiritual struggles of the two young men, one rebelling in vain, the other clearly overwhelmed, are evident. The *Moses* (figs. 31-32) also for the sepulchre, accompanied them, as imposing and formidable as the Sistine Prophets. Michelangelo was often accused of inactivity on the Tomb – he certainly experienced innumerable delays – and it was many years later (perhaps around 1532) that he sketched out the four *Prisoners* now at the Accademia (figs. 33-36). The struggle for freedom from their tragic imprisonment in the rough-hewn block is clear. The *Victory* (fig. 51, today in the Palazzo Vecchio) shows the young conqueror standing over his subdued foe, depressed and anguished, perhaps conscious of the futility of it all. The beautiful figure is a complex contortion, a spiralling composition often called serpentine. It is far away from the serene confidence of the *David* (figs. 10-11), and the aesthetic requirements are now much changed.

In Florence, during the second decade of the sixteenth century, Medici rule was re-established. The new Pope, Leo X, who had known Michelangelo for a long time, was also a Medici, but chose to employ him not in Rome, where Raphael held sway, but in Florence. In 1516 Michelangelo was commissioned to plan the *facade of the Medici Basilica of San Lorenzo*, a model of which exists in Casa Buonarroti (compare fig. 52). This he designed in his usual monumental way, a blend of architecture and sculpture, which would involve years of quarrying marble in Versilia. This project was never realised, through lack of adequate funds, and was replaced (from 1520) by the New Sacristy of San Lorenzo, a Medici funerary chapel. Michelangelo negotiated principally with Cardinal Giulio dei Medici, the future Pope Clement VII, who allowed Buonarroti to realise his plans, even when problems intervened, by giving him substantial freedom of action: "he says he knows your vision is greater than his is; he will leave you alone in your work".

The *Sacristy* (figs. 39-40) should have been a funerary chapel of the Medici, who had by then acquired princely and papal status. It was to house the bodies of Lorenzo the Magnificent and his brother Giuliano (who was assassinated in the Pazzi conspiracy); Giuliano, Duke of Nemours (who died in 1516) and Lorenzo, Duke of Urbino (died 1519), two Medici princes whose promise came to nothing; finally, the bodies of the Popes Leo X and Clement VII.

Michelangelo, however, rose above the self-indulgent pomposity of the theme, and managed to express more weighty universal values. He also resurrected the plan for Brunelleschi's Old Sacristy, thereby linking with an earlier, more sedate Florentine tradition. Then, in the *statuary*, rather than glorifying power, he chose to reflect on human destiny and futility, as if to appease his idealism (figs. 41-2, 45-6). Condivi in his day said that "Time devours all things". A current interpretation (Tolnay) sees in the Chapel a symbolic representation of the Universe with its three hemispheres, one above the other. Of the three architectural divisions, the lower with the tombs would represent the Hades of the dead; the middle, where the architecture is more restrained and rational, the terrestrial sphere; the top, high and light, with its lunettes, dome and radial coffering, the celestial vault. The pairs of statues crowning the tombs (*Day* and *Night*, *Dawn* and *Dusk*) symbolise the inexorable passing of time leading to death; the break in the centre of the tomb lids perhaps signifies that "the immortal spirit of the deceased (the two princes) is liberated, to rise up to a state inaccesible to the blind forces of time". The Spirit there rediscovers its essential self "through the eternal contemplation of the meaning of life, symbolised by the Virgin and Child". Both statues of the Princes in fact look towards this sculpture, which is placed at the side in front of the altar. Other interpretations have been proposed, but the powerful, grave, pained figures of the Hours and the brooding demeanour of the two Princes undoubtedly signify a solemn view of death. There is a famous story that when an observer noted that his statue did not resemble the Duke Giuliano, Michelangelo replied that no-one would know how he looked in a thousand years time. Indeed, the idealism distilled in the statues of the New Sacristy is such that one can read into them many conflicting intentions and themes. Is Giuliano, for example, the strong-willed and violent despot, or the anti-Machiavellian prince, a model of moral rectitude? Is he the handsome *vir activus*, or an irresolute consumptive? Clearly, the same psychological signposts can lead to ambiguity and different conclusions. To this set also belong the *Kneeling Youth* (fig. 50), now in St. Petersburg (the attribution of which is not secure) and the *Fiume* (fig. 49), of which there is a model in Casa Buonarroti.

Many things changed over the fifteen or so years that this work took. Michelangelo had started under the patronage of the Medicis, but they were overthrown in 1527 by Republicans, after Rome had undergone a terrible and profane sacking. Florence was then dominated by the Imperial armies. We must not, however, overlook the *Risen Christ* (fig. 37) of which Michelangelo produced a second version for the Roman Metello Vari in 1519-21. This work again reflects something of ancient sculpture, and combines pagan forms of statuary, like the Greco-Roman styles, with Christian images (the Cross, etc.). It also draws on Leonardo to some degree.

From 1523, Michelangelo was also working on a new commission: the *Biblioteca Laurenziana* in Florence, part of the convent of San Lorenzo. Finished much later, the Biblioteca is an example,

Madonna suckling her Child.

Cleopatra.

along with the Sacristy, of a new architectural vision. In the *Vestibule* (fig. 53), the staircase breaks out in a cascade, and the columns seem to have been hewn from the walls in a style that anticipates the Baroque. The long reading-room, with its special desks for the precious codices, is heavily decorated. One can also perceive symbolism in the relationship between the Vestibule, naturally lower, seemingly restless, and the higher reading-room: "the contrast between the two rooms reflects the struggles and aspirations of the outside world (Vestibule) with the orderly pursuit of studies, theorising and literary leisure in the upper level (reading-room)" (De Angelis d'Ossat).

MICHELANGELO IN THE DEFENCE AND DEFEAT OF HIS CITY:
The Fortifications of Florence - The Apollo-David

Omitting other minor works, we move on to 1527 with the sack of Rome, the fall of the Medicis and the return of the old Republic in Florence. Michelangelo, who was essentially a Republican, put himself at their disposal, assuming control of the fortifications, for which he was nominated Governor at the beginning of 1529. That summer he was invited on a mission to Ferrara to study their fortification, and he there promised Duke Alfonso a cartoon for a Leda (lost but recorded in replicas). To defend the gates of Florence, he then designed unique bastions, reminiscent of crustaceans, with 'trunnions' and *Bulwarks* (fig. 54). Some judge that he was involved in the development of heavy artillery, but contemporary critics testify that they had little practical success. Rumours of treachery and defeat dismayed Buonarroti, however, and that September he fled to Venice. In Florence, however, which was under siege, he was condemned. Michelangelo soon returned, though, and his subsequent behaviour was courageous. When, in August 1530, Florence capitulated, he hid himself in the tower of S. Niccolò and the police searched his house in vain.

Pope Clement pardoned Michelangelo, who returned to work on the sculptures for the New Sacristy (1530-34) "prompted more by fear than choice" (Condivi). He bitterly attacked the marble with an aggression that gave rise to fears for his health. His friend, Sebastian del Piombo wrote to him in 1531: "I'm told that you are working day and night"; and shortly afterwards that "when (Clement VII) read your letter to me, he was amazed that the figures were finished. He said that he'd never known a harder worker than you, to beg you to take it easier, to do only what you can, so there would be no disruption, no illness... He said you should go for a walk sometimes..." Michelangelo also had a sculpture to produce for the stern Baccio Valori, the Papal Commissary. This was the *Apollo-David* (fig. 38), today in the Bargello, a delicate 'serpentine' figure. There was also the cartoon 'Noli Me Tangere' for the Marchese del Vasto, and a 'Venus and Cupid' for his friend Bartolomeo Bettini (known from copies). We also have records of a new contract in 1532 for the tomb of Julius II, and from that period also come the four Prisoners now in the Accademia, and the Victory in the Palazzo Vecchio.

MICHELANGELO LEAVES FLORENCE:
The Last Judgement - Brutus.

Michelangelo's father died, aged 91, in 1534. Fearful of the young, hostile Duke Alessandro, Michelangelo left Florence for good, and moved to Rome. Clement VII's successor, Paul III Farnese (1534-39) was a lover of art, and warmly received the more eminent Florentine exiles. Here was the handsome nobleman Tommaso Cavalieri, for whom Michelangelo developed a real attachment; here also he would have met Vittoria Colonna. Aged 60, Michelangelo wrote letters and platonic love-poems to Cavalieri, and drew detailed sketches on mythological themes that mirrored his own feelings: Ganymede, Tityus, The Fall of Phaeton, Archers, Bacchanalia, and a 'Divine Head' – all because Cavalieri was "learning to draw". This fascination with Cavalieri was one of the reasons he settled in Rome.

Pope Paul III, meanwhile, commissioned two major frescoes for the Sistine Chapel. The Fall of the Rebel Angels was to have been on the entrance wall, but was never carried out; on the other, the *Last Judgement* (figs. 56-58). The cartoons for this were ready in 1535; the painting, produced solely by Michelangelo, was unveiled on All-Hallow's Eve, 1541. The fresco was received with unreserved hyperbole, though there were some reservation about the total nudity and various other points. N. Sernini, for example, wrote to a Cardinal: "a great and difficult work, with seemingly more than five hundred figures (actually just under four hundred) of a king that no other painter can match. Even if it were as beautiful as you say, there are still plenty who condemn it. Indeed, the Very Reverend Order of the Chietini object to nudes in such a place; others complain that Christ has no beard and is too young..." Above all, the malicious Pietro Aretino, offended because Michelangelo had not followed his advice about the composition, pretended to be scandalised, writing to him "such figures are better suited to the baths (a place of pleasures) than amongst the heavenly chorus..." Indeed, in 1564, it was ordered that the 'obscene' parts of the pictures should be covered up.

In reality, though, nothing could have been more unaffected and dramatic than Michelangelo's vision. From the striking pose of an athletic Christ, shown young and beardless like an Apollo, the scene acquires a swirling motion, with large groups of figures floating in empty space like storm clouds gathering for the Apocalypse. Below and to the left, serenaded by a host of trumpeting angels, the dead are awakening to a new life, some magically drawn by divine force towards the heavens; others, already damned, falling into the depths of despair. Here, the boat of Charon ferries its load of sinners towards the abyss. In the right hand corner stands Minos. Alternatively, high up in the lunette, swirling angels carry symbols of Christ's Passion, as a repentance for human conscience. The Apostles, Martyrs and Saints are pressing in a mass around Christ, alongside whom the Virgin cowers. On the skin held by St. Batholomew is the painter's grotesque self-portrait. The two dominant colours of the Sistine Vault are the

Study for A Risen Christ.

brown of the bodies on the background of the sky. The perspective is dramatic (the higher figures are actually 2.5 metres high, the lower ones 1.55 metres). The powerful anatomical forms seem rather resigned to their spiritual destiny; the beauty of line and shape create a powerful harmony, Highlighting the drama of the scene. Even as the accusations of heresy mounted, Michelangelo was feeling the religious dichotomy for himself: the anguish of the sinner, and the wonder of the Divine. In his own way, he was a participant in the Judgement, and lived for it, having little time for anything else. When, later, Daniele da Volterra was ordered by Pope Paul IV to cover up the more scabrous nudity, Buonarroti sarcastically commented that "His Holiness obviously intends to put the world to rights, since arranging the painting is such a small contribution".

During the work on the Last Judgement, Michelangelo also sculpted the bust of 'Brutus' (today at the Bargello, fig. 55). It was instigated for Cardinal Ridolfi by the exiled politician and man of letters Donato Giannotti. It is a portrait of a tyrant, haughty and aggressive in profile, inspired by the ancient Imperial busts, especially that of Caracalla. It has been suggested that it was an idealised portrait of Lorenzino dei Medici; he had killed the Duke Alessandro in 1537 in Florence, attracting all the anti-Medici sympathisers to his cause.

THE PAINTINGS AND SCULPTURES OF HIS OLD AGE:
*The Conversion of Paul - The Crucifixion of Peter - The Florence Pietà -
The Palestrina Pietà - The Rondanini Pietà.*

From 1542-45, the tomb of Julius II was finally completed and placed in San Pietro in Vincoli. It was the sixth successive scheme, and much reduced in scale; the Slaves were no longer part of it, nor the Victory. Only the gigantic Moses, flanked by 'Rachel' and 'Leah' remained - there is undoubtedly a certain coldness about these works-plus other figures by helpers. Between 1542 and 1550, Buonarroti produced, within the Pauline Chapel, two large frescoes: the *Conversion of Paul* and the *Crucifixion of Peter* (figs. 59-60). The first is similar in style to the Last Judgement, yet both display a dynamism which is perplexing, notwithstanding recent calls for a reevaluation of these intense works. They certainly reflect the crisis of personality that the elderly Michelangelo was now experiencing. The influence of Vittoria Colonna and her circle amounted to a 'conversion', a search not for outward fulfillment, but more a spiritual and inward-looking examination. It has been said that these last two frescoes portray two moments of the test of personal faith: conversion and martyrdom.

Colonna died in 1547. Her circle eschewed the reformist religious ideals of Valdès, Ochino and others, namely in justification through faith alone, rather than the salvation of the soul through virtuous acts. Michelangelo subscribed to these ideals, already being reflected in his poetry:

"To ascend without grace is a thought in vain..."

He felt that the spirit was unable to attain fulfillment without divine intervention:

*"I love you (O God) with my tongue
And then I mourn that love does not reach the heart;
Neither do I know well from where
The door opens to Grace...
From when the pen does not correspond
To the work and makes the page a liar".*

It should be noted here that Michelangelo still allowed for charitable works to the poor, furnishing dowries to girls without means, for example.

This sense of an almost desperate religious anxiety is further expressed in drawings like the beautiful late series (about 1555) for a Crucifixion – developed from an earlier set on the same theme produced for Vittoria Colonna, but now lost – and in the sculptural groupings of the three Pietàs.

The *Florence Pietà* dates from about 1550-55 (figs. 61-62) and was originally created by Michelangelo for his tomb in Santa Maria Maggiore in Rome. It was subsequently mutilated by other artists and completed by Calcagni, to whom we owe the finishing touches of the Magdalen. The figure of Christ is bent, as if broken, at the leg and His arms extend in a disjointed arch, supported by a roughly-sketched Madonna and a kneeling Magdalen. Atop the angular grouping we see the hooded figure of Joseph of Arimathea – a portrait of Michelangelo himself. The fact that the artist stands so

The Sacrifice of Abraham.

Drawing of the Crucified Christ.

close to Christ is deliberate; this notion dominated his thinking. There is a famous anecdote about a night-time visit made by Vasari, in Rome, to the old man, who was actually sculpting this Pieta at the time. Giving his customary knock, the door was openedand Michelangelo appeared with a lamp in his hand. Vasari explained the request, on the Pope's behalf, for a drawing. Michelangelo then sent the faithful Urbino upstairs. Vasari, meanwhile, caught sight of a leg from the group on which Michelangelo was working and making some alterations. Instantly secretive about the work in hand, the artist pretended to drop the lantern, and they were left in darkness. He then called Urbino to fetch a light; meanwhile he drew Vasari away from the statue and commented: "I am so old that death often tugs at my cloak for me to go with him. One day my body will fall just like that lamp, and my light will be put out".

The *Palestrina Pietà* (fig. 63) now in the Accademia, is not recorded in early documents and is not accepted as genuine by a number of scholars. The powerful reclining body of the dead Christ is supported with seeming difficulty by his two grieving attendants. The figures adopt an essentially parallel stance, as can be seen in the Pauline Chapel. Finally, the *Rondanini pietà* (fig. 70), in Sforzesco Castle Museum, was described in the inventory of Michelangelo's Roman house as "another statue of a Christ with another figure above, joined together, sketched out and unfinished". The artist had worked on it until the eve of his death, changing the composition in various ways; the right arm being left unattached to the body, for example. There is in Oxford a drawing of the first design for this statue. The Rondanini Pietà displays a quality both medieval yet modern, which locks the work into its time as a Renaissance work of art. It's expressiveness is of the spirit; the two exhausted figures almost fuse together in their shared experience.

THE ROMAN ARCHITECTURE AND THE END:
The Piazza del Campidoglio - St. Peter's - The Last Works.

Towards the middle of the century, Michelangelo had also carried out great architectural works. From 1546, there was the completion of the Farnese Palace (the impressive exterior cornices, and the third floor of the courtyard, which is significantly more dynamic than the earlier two by Sangallo). That same year, the laying out of the Piazza del Campidoglio commenced (notably the use of the gigantic Corinthian pilasters, and the powerful harmony within the Piazza with its central equestrian statue). From 1547, he was the chief architect of St. Peter's, and so it was that the church in which he had been unable to site the sepulchre of Jiulis II, and in which he had seen Bramante triumph, finished in his hands. Yet he now recognised the genius of the Bramante project – "clear, open and bright" – and had to compete with its fraudulent successors, the Sangallo set. Buonarroti wanted to return to the Greek cross, reducing the peripheral areas with a colossal pilaster order above, plus an attic. In the facade there would have been a portico and a pronaos. Four minor domes would have offset the main cupola with a double-domed effect like that in Florence, but shaped and detailed differently. It was also to have been originally hemispheric in shape, but was later modified by Della Porta.

Meanwhile, one new Pope followed another, and Michelangelo lived modestly in the small house at Macel dei Corvi. Here he waited for a death that would not come, a death which he had depicted in a painting at the top of the stairs in his house. He was subsequently afflicted by gallstones. While Julius III was Pope (1550-55), Buonarroti worked on projects for San Giovanni dei Fiorentini, and proposed to Ignatius di Loyola that he handle the work for the Church of Gesù, 'just for devotion'. Under Pope Paul IV (1555-59) a strict counter-reformation developed, and the Inquisition threatened. The nudity of the Last Judgement in the Sistine Chapel was painted over. Michelangelo was even accused of being a Lutheran. Under the patronage of Pius IV (1559-65), however, other architectural commissions were entrusted to Buonarroti: the reconstruction of the gates into Rome, of which only the *Porta Pia* ever materialised, in 1561 (fig. 69); the transformation of the Diocletian Baths into the Church and Convent of Santa Maria degli Angeli (1536-66), and the Sforza Chapel (1564). Michelangelo rose at sunrise to start work, and was still working late at night, attacking the marblee with incredible force. He would work from the light of a candle fixed to a cardboard hat on his head. At the age of eighty-one he wrote to Vasari that it was midnight, that death was sculpted in every one of his thoughts, and that he was unable to return to Florence while the work on St. Peter's continued, even though there were many who wanted to take over from him. He would quote - even though "many say I am in my second childhood" – the very beautiful sonnet which begins:

"My span of life has run its course...".

and ends:

*"There's no painting or sculpture now that quiets
The soul that's pointed toward that holy Love
That on the cross opened Its arms to take us".*

On 14th January 1564, aged nearly ninety, he became ill, dying at sunset on the 18th. Tommaso Cavalieri, Daniele da Volterra and two doctors were present. The body, taken to S.S. Apostoli in Rome, was almost immediately removed, and secretly taken back by his nephew to Florence, where it arrived on March 10th, causing a considerable stir. On July 14th, the Academy of Drawing celebrated his funeral in San Lorenzo, the Medici church. In 1570, his monumental tomb in San Croce, designed by Vasari and built by others, was completed.

1 - *Madonna of the Steps* (Florence - Casa Buonarroti).

2 - *Battle of the Centaurs* (Florence - Casa Buonarroti).

3 - *Angel with Candelabrum*
(Bologna - San Domenico).

4 - *Crucifix*
(Florence - Casa Buonarroti).

5 - *Bacchus* (Florence - Bargello National Museum).

6 - *Bruges Madonna* (Bruges - Nôtre Dame).

7 - *Pietà* (Rome - St. Peter's).

8 - *Pietà* - Detail of the *Face of the Madonna.*

9 - The *Tribuna*
(Florence - Galleria
dell'Accademia).

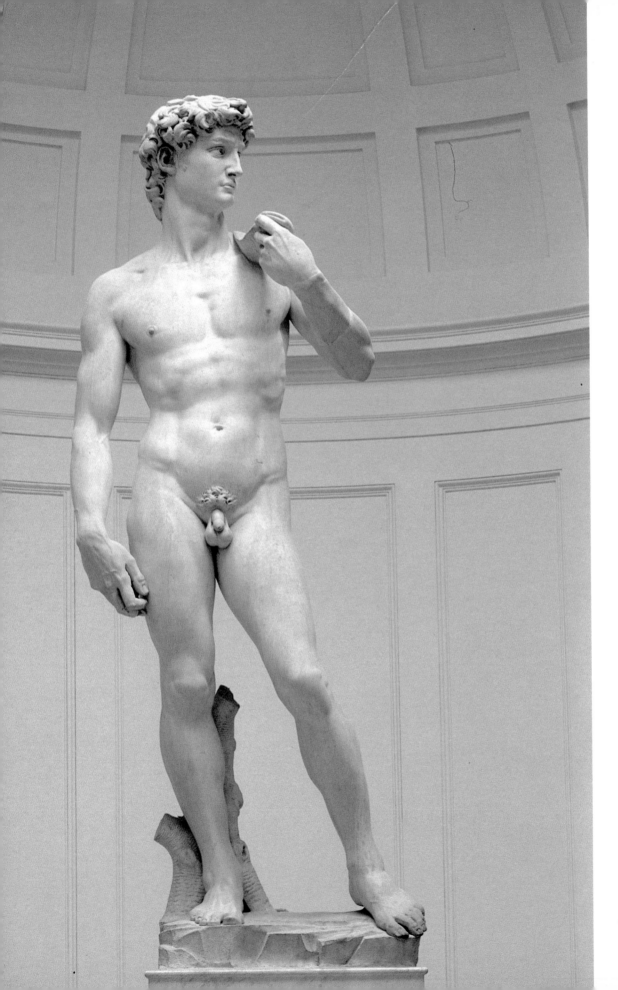

10-11 - *David*
(Florence -
Galleria
dell'Accademia).

12 - *Pitti Tondo* (Florence - Bargello National Museum)

13 - *Doni Tondo* (Florence - Uffizi Gallery).

14 - *Taddei Tondo* (London - Royal Academy).

15 - *St. Matthew*
(Florence - Galleria dell'Accademia).

16. – General view of the vault of the restored *Sistine Chapel*.

17. – Restored Sistine Chapel – *The Original Sin* and *the Expulsion from Paradise*.

18. – Restored Sistine Chapel – *The Creation of Man*.

19. – Restored Sistine Chapel – *The Creation of Woman* (detail).

20. - Sistine Chapel - *The Prophet Daniel*   21. - Sistine Chapel - *The Libyan Sibyl*

LIBICA

DELPHICA

22. - Sistine Chapel - *The Delphic Sibyl*

IOEL

23. - Sistine Chapel - *The Prophet Joel*

24. - Sistine Chapel - *The Erythraean Sibyl*

25. - Sistine Chapel - *The Prophet Zachariah*

26. - Sistine Chapel - *The Cumaean Sibyl*

27. - Sistine Chapel - *The Prophet Ezekiel*

28. - *Dying Prisoner* (Paris - Louvre) 29. - *Rebelling Prisoner* (Paris - Louvre)

30. - *Tomb of Julius II* (Rome - San Pietro in Vincoli). In the centre
the *Moses,* at the sides the statues of *Rachel* (right) and *Lea* (left)

31.-32. - *The Moses* ▶

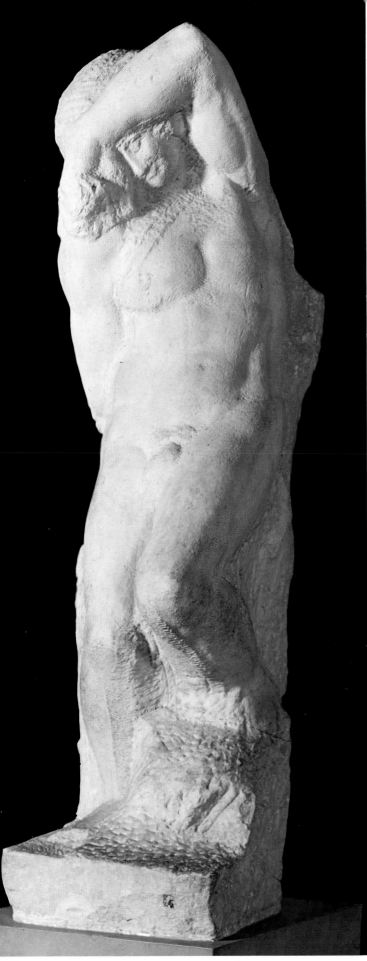

33. *The youthful Prisoner*

34 *The bearded Prisoner*

(QUI PERVENNE DALLA GROTTA DEL BUONTALENTI
IN BOBOLI NEL LUGLIO 1909)

MICHELANGIOLO
ABBOZZO DI UN «PRIGIONE»
PAPA GIULIO II

35. - *Prisoner called « Atlantis »*

(QUI PERVENNE DALLA GROTTA DEL BUONTALENTI
IN BOBOLI NEL LUGLIO 1909)

MICHELANGIOLO
«PRIGIONE»

36 - *Awakening Prisoner*

38. - *The David Apollo*
(Florence - Bargello National Museaum)

37 - *Christ Risen* (or *Bearing the Cross*)
(Rome - Santa Maria sopra Minerva)

39. 40. General view of the *New Sacristy* in San Lorenzo (Florence)

41.-42. - *Statue and Tomb of Lorenzo, Duke of Urbino* (The New Sacristy)

43. - Tomb of Lorenzo - *Statue of Evening*

44. - Tomb of Lorenzo - *Statue of Dawn*

45.-46. - *Statue and Tomb of Giuliano, Duke of Nemours (The New Sacristy)*

47. - Tomb of Giuliano - *Statue of Night*

48. - Tomb of Giuliano - *Statue of Day*

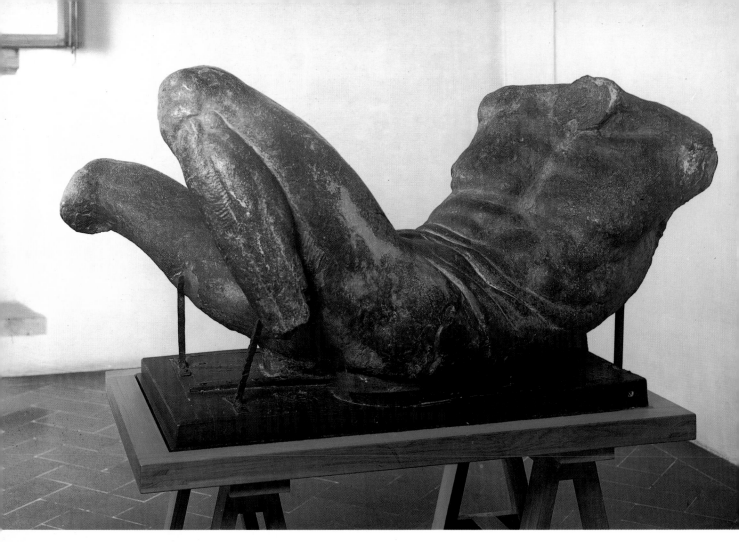

49. - *Model of River* (Florence - Buonarroti House)

50. - *Inclining Youth*
(Leningrado - The Eremitage)

51. - *The Victory*
(Florence - The Palazzo Vecchio)

53. - *Hall and stairs of the Laurenziana Library* (Florence)

52. - *Model for the façade of the Church of San Lorenzo* (Florence - Buonarroti House)

54. - *Drawing for the fortifications of Florence* (Florence - Buonarroti House)

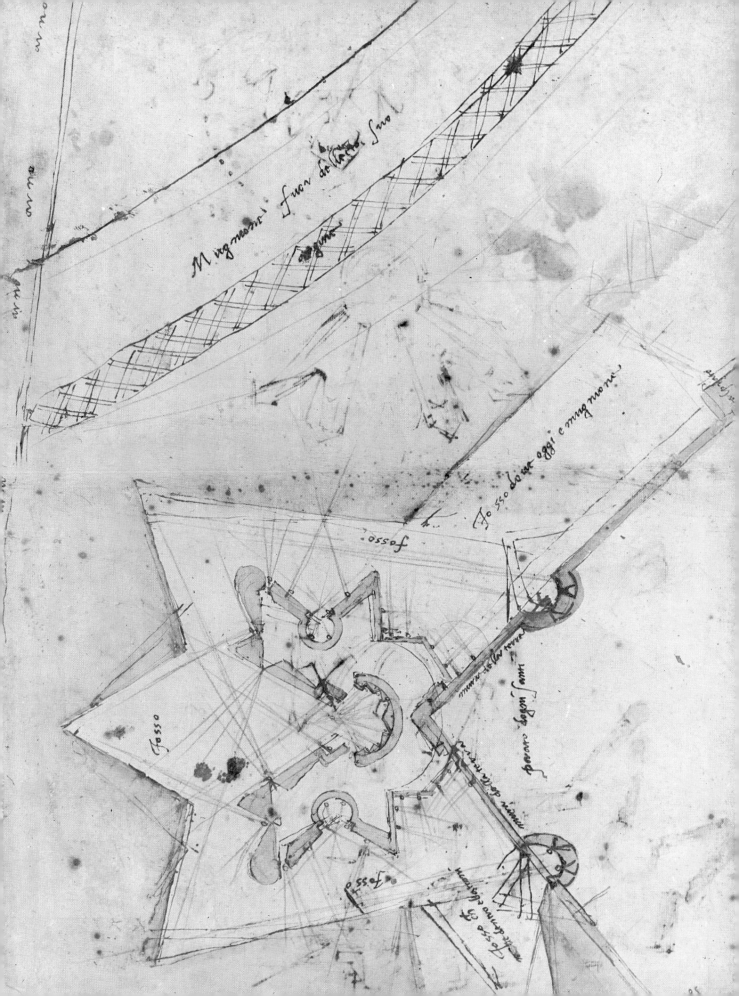

55. - *Bust of Brutus* (Florence - Bargello National Museum)

56. - *The Last Judgment* (Sistine Chapel - Vatican Museums)

57. - Detail of the *Last Judgment*

58. - *Christ the Judge* - Detail of the Last Judgment

59. - *The Fall of St. Paul* (The Paolina Chapel - Vatican Museums)

60 - *Crucifixion of St. Peter* (The Paolina Chapel - Vatican Museums).

61.-62. - *Pietà* (Opera del Duomo Museum - Florence,
previously in the Cathedral of Santa Maria del Fiore).

63. - *The Pietà of Palestrina* (Florence - Academy Gallery)

64.-65. - *Michelangelo's plan for the systematization of the Campidoglio reppresented in two etchings of 1567 and 1568*

66. - *Drawing for the plan of the Church of San Giovanni dei Florentines in Rome (Florence - Buonarroti House)*

67. - *Courtyard of the Farnese Palace in an etching of 1560*

68. - *Dome of St. Peter's Basilica*

69. - *Drawing for the Porta Pia in Rome* (Florence - Buonarroti House)

70. - *Rondanini Pietà* (Milan - Sforzesco Castle).